Fragments of My Soul

Brian Roberts

BookLeaf Publishing

Presentation by *BookLeaf Publishing*

Web: www.bookleafpub.com

E-mail: info@bookleafpub.com

ISBN: 9789357618182

First edition 2022

To my best friend and muse Chase, who inspired me to live my truth and be myself, love myself for who I am, and live life for myself instead of others- you have done more for me in 3 years than most people in my life have ever done, though you may not realize it. Your spirit and energy are inspiring and uplifting, a beacon of light in the darkness at times. Your pragmatic outlook on life, nonjudgmental advice, bright smile, and warm hug is always there when I need it. I'm not sure how among the billions of people on this planet I got lucky enough to stumble into you and make our paths cross, but life has been better because of it. Here's to the adventures and experiences we've had, and to our future plans and worldwide adventures to come. I look forward to seeing where the road of life takes us. This one is for you.

ACKNOWLEDGEMENT

I would be seriously remiss if I failed to acknowledge a few individuals who helped inspire me throughout life and give me the confidence to believe in myself, and the courage to publish this book: Joel Lewis, my guidance counselor in the group home who introduced me to Ginsburg. Eliot Wilson at CU Denver, who inspired me with his writings and words of encouragement when reviewing my works. Bronson and Desiree, two of my best friends in life who have always been there for me for the last 15+ years on this roller coaster of life. And last but not least, my grandmother Patricia and my aunt Ann who have always been there for me through the ups and downs of life, family issues, a tumultuous childhood, and my adult life, never judging me and always there to lift me up, though the good choices and the bad.

PREFACE

"Poetry and Hums aren't things which you get, they're things which get you. And all you can do is to go where they can find you." — A.A. Milne, The House at Pooh Corner

I've always been an ambitious reader, starting with my first book at the age of four, and haven't put down any books since. It gave me an appetite for knowledge, adventure, fantasy, and wanderlust that has yet to be sated no matter how many words I consume. I've found in life that poetry speaks to me on another level, because often in brevity so much emotion can still be conveyed in an easily digestible format without being as intimidating in length as a novel. Writers like Poe, Ginsburg, and Plath all spoke to my soul as I read their words, inspiring me to want to move people with my words to experience those same emotions those writers made me feel. Writers like David Sedaris showed me it was possible to be introspective on your life experiences, good and bad, and look back on life with bemusement and a wry smile, despite some of the challenges one may face and survive, in an honest, raw, inspirational way.

And so in the style of Winnie the Pooh, I've traveled the world and experienced the many ups and downs of life, putting myself in places and situations in which poetry and hums found me, and I decided to share glimpses into those moments in the hopes that you may share in my journey, through the good and the bad, while also using this collection of poems as a cathartic exercise to exorcise many of the things I have kept bottled up inside all these years. I welcome you to join me for a glimpse into my soul, and hope you find something that resonates with you.

Mindfreak

Come little children, so sweet and dear
Take a walk through my mind-enter through my
ear.
Beyond the canal, past the drum
Buckle up kiddos this ride will be fun.

To the left my marbles, I'm losing them fast
Let's enter my subconscious- this should be a
blast.
Homicidal, suicidal, sexual thoughts abound-
Are you starting to realize my mind is unsound?

The ride's moving faster the deeper we go
To the farthest recesses, now let's take it slow.
A graveyard of brain cells, all of them fried
The booze and drugs to kill my pain are the
reason they died.

A triple locked and bolted door is all that
remains
But your tour ends here, no time to explain.
Better some things are locked away for me to
handle alone
So scurry along, and head back to your home

It was a short little mindfuck
I’m so glad you came
Am I really that nuts?
Am I going insane?

A Night At The Ward

The door creaks
The floor squeaks
Someone's tapping on my door
A raven cries out "Nevermore!"

As the thunder claps outside
I wonder how to save my precious hide
As I lay under the covers and cower
I hope to survive the witching hour

Loud long moans echo off the walls
Chains are rattling in the halls
Shadows dance around the room
I feel a sense of impending doom

Ghouls trying to break down the door
Mice scurry around the floor
My mind filled with wonder, my heart with fright
For I'm trapped in the nightmare on Halloween night

I hear a heartbeat in the air
Jacob Marley's in my chair
The raven continues to fly freely about

All this terror I could do without

I don't remember my bed ever talking
And now the dresser is up and walking
As they approach my bed I shout out for a sword
That I may defend this mental ward

The doctor says I'm very insane
I beg to differ, I'm ahead of the game
For all these "figments" in my head
Have made the poor man rather dead

And I'm next

Aftermath

The stench of death still fills the air
Permeating every cell of the building and my skin.

There is no escaping it, it fills every orifice

A hazy cloud settling over the neighborhood as the streets are quiet
Aside from the occasional wailing of sirens as they cart the bodies to the morgue

I look out my window and see the smoldering ruins

I close my eyes and hear the sounds of objects echoing off the sidewalk

THWACK, THUMP, CRASH, a dull sickening hollow sound

Like a wet bag of sand hitting the pavement

It became impossible to tell the difference between the sound of flesh or concrete striking the pavement

Watching the first building rise up in flames
after hearing the roar of the impact on the tower

Standing on the roof watching the second crash
into its twin

The city I loved burning, the chaos unfolding
before my very eyes.

Running toward the area to provide whatever
help I could, but what could I do?

How does one even begin to help, what good
does a bottle of water, or wet rags do to help
those running through the clouds and debris
fields down the street

Wailing, crying, screaming, everyone with a
dead hollow look in their eyes, trying to process
the horrors unfolding.

Watching the towers fall, watching the cloud of
dust pouring down the street, fleeing with the
masses as if Godzilla had invaded Tokyo, but
this creature was real

This was no radioactive accident, this was
hatred, this was terror, this was war.

I must remind myself not of the horrors of that
day, as I sit here looking out my window a few
miles away a week later,

Watching the ruins smolder and I inhale the
fumes, wondering if that is the smell of asbestos
or charred flesh, wondering how long it can
continue to burn

No, we must not remember the sights we cannot
unsee
The sounds we will never stop hearing.

Instead we must remember the brave, those who
gave their lives that others may live.

Those who defied the face of terror and spat in
it, who showed what true grit and resolve were

Fathers of friends, coworkers, strangers, all who
gave the entirety of themselves to rescue
countless others

As a city, as a country, we bent, but did not
break.

They wanted to break our spirit, but they
strengthened it instead.

We banded together, united as one, black, white, brown, Christian, Jew, Hindu,
We stood in unity, stared down the belly of the beast.

And that is what I need to focus on, to remember, both in that moment as the smells filled the air around me in my room

And even now decades later at night when the smells and sounds come back to pay a visit.

Surely if the towers and nation can be rebuilt, unwavering, unbending, unbreakable,

So too can I be the same, and not give in to the darkness and horrors that remain in the recesses of my mind trying to creep out.

Instead we will lock those away in the abyss, with the doors shored up by remembering the helpers, as Mr. Rogers would say.

Bayley

Furry brown loaf, laying there without a care in the world
Eat, sleep, snore, repeat, it's an idyllic life.
No responsibility, no pain, not heartbreak, no heartache
Just snore, lick, bark, chew, woof, sleep, repeat.

And still, this lethargic critter laying at my feed has helped me as much as I've helped her.
Those lonely nights when she can sense I am down, and saunters over to give a nudge with her nose
Carrying the one toy she likes in her mouth to bring to me
Because it's her favorite thing that makes her happy and she wants to share that joy

Did she rescue me or did I rescue her?
It seems cliché, but it's true.
Of all the animals in those cages, barking, yapping, crying out for attention
Our eyes locked and you sat there quiet, stoic, resolute, with a look of hurt and neglect in your eyes

And in that moment I felt a kindred spirit, for I too had that same look and dim light behind darkened eyes.
I too had come from a broken past.
And when you came out of the cage and immediately wrapped those paws around my waits in a hig and licked my face I knew you were the one.
You were like me, broken, but undeterred, desperate to share what love you still had with someone else, despite out broken pasts.

You came home the same day, and we've been side by side ever since, through ups and downs, Through car crashes, heartbreak, on road trips, in an ever changing world filled with rancor and chaos, you've always been the steady absolute.
No longer underfed, riddled with worms and Lyme disease, no longer abandoned and abused.

In those first few months we healed each other- I mended your body, you mended my spirit.
You remain the constant in my life, and I dread the day you cross the rainbow bridge, where Hobo will be waiting to greet you while you both wait for me.
But until that day comes, I am fur-ever grateful we found each other, two kindred spirits fated to meet.

Cat's Cradle

I thought of you today and laughed to myself-
Not even my cancer is good enough for you.
But nothing in my life ever was, so why should
it start now?
You always made me feel like a disappointment
Maybe I am, I can't even get the right type of
cancer
To make you care enough to pull your head out
of your ass and care to try and mend fences

You never wanted me- I was an artifact, a relic
from a failed marriage
A constant reminder of your troubled past, an
anchor weighing you down
Perhaps it would have been better had you
aborted me
And spared me from the life of pain you and her
cursed me with

I was the third wheel for your new life
I was the shit stain on the carpet of your new
home
I was the hole in the white picket fence
The gopher eating through your new garden

I was the hot potato to be passed back and forth between you and her
Neither wanted me, you just tolerated me for brief periods
Subjecting me to various abuses- mental, emotional, physical
You provided me with an endless buffet
Each of you with your own unique way of serving them up

And yet from childhood until now I still tried
In some strange Stockholm syndrome type of way to win your love, your affection
To feel like I mattered, to feel like you cared.
But nothing was ever good enough.
A 96 on a test should have been 100.
Trying to relive your life to win your approval and yet you never noticed
I never wanted to play in the band, but I did it because you were in it.
I never wanted to run track, but I did it because you did.
I hated sports, but endured it because you'd pay attention to me, even if it was to tell me what I did wrong.
I spouted your Stormfront-esque political views without forging my own, but you never cared.

You were never there for me when I needed a
defender.
I was bullied and harassed in grade school, and
you were embarrassed for yourself because I
was weak
You tried to teach me to stand up for myself and
gave up trying because I was too soft
You threw me out and locked me away so that
you could live your perfect Stepford life
Blaming my anger but never asking why I was
so mad because you never cared.

Forcing me to go back to the school where my
attackers were waiting like sharks who saw
chum in the water
But you had me so fearful and terrified of you I
couldn't tell you what happened to me
How they held me down and had their way with
me and joked about it for years afterward
And how that's why I was so angry and the
outbursts escalated
And maybe if you had cared I you could have
helped or interceded
But instead it was easier to discard me like
yesterday's garbage

You've always shown disdain for me
And when you're gone and I try my best to think
of happy memories

I fear instead I will only remember the yelling, the spanking, the punching, the cd player being broken over my head
The look of guacamole and ground meat being shoved into your cheek at 12am as I sit in the bar humiliated the night before graduation trying to sober you up
The fact you hated your family so much you needed to be drunk to be around us, and that you almost slept your hangover off and missed my graduation, because you never gave a shit about me
You were only there out of obligation.

And I got tired- I can't do this anymore.
And so I cut ties. This had nothing to do with politics.
Nothing to do with who I loved.
But it did have everything to do with a systemic pattern of abuse over 3 decades of life
Of the pressure of trying to live up to an unrealistic standard
Of seeking approval I would never get, like Sisyphus rolling the boulder uphill
I reached my breaking point- It had to be you or me before I drove myself insane
And so I decided to be like you- To cast you aside, to shed you from my life so that I can try to find my happiness

Like you did to me all those years ago.

So maybe the apple doesn't fall far from the tree.
And one day perhaps you'll realize it's too late
and feel some regret
That the cat is in the cradle with the silver spoon
And your boy grew up like you
Your boy was just like you.

Distance

I wish that I could tell you, I wish that you could see
Just how much I love you and what you mean to me.

I love you like the tides love the moon,
You stay in my orbit and pull and affect me through highs and lows
I love you like the grass loves the sun
Reaching out despite you being distant and unobtainable, yet your warmth still nurtures me

I love you like the bees love nectar
Your sweetness sustains me, and give me life, helping me transform it into something greater in myself
I love you like the flames love the air
Feeding me with spark, a slow burn with whispered words, burning hotter and brighter when you come on strong

I love you like the sky loves the stars
Your brightness shining in the darkness, lighting the way, a beautiful canvas that inspires my dreams

I love you like the ships love the ocean
Vast, deep, nurturing, rough, powerful, moving,
endless and full of possibilities and new
frontiers.

I love you like Romeo loved Juliet
Forbidden, irresistible, willing to die for a
chance with you.
And until I fall upon my sword and bare my
chest for that chance
I will continue to love you from afar.

Echoes of The Past

Sitting in the darkness, wishing I could sleep
Trying so damn hard not to lay on the couch and weep
I wish I could silence these thoughts running through my mind
Desperately seeking out the inner peace I can't find

I just feel so empty, hopeless and dead inside
I have no ego, self-esteem or sense of pride
I try to feel wanted by hooking up online
Being used and cast aside only buys me a little more time

I know I can't fill the void with casual fun
But what are you supposed to do when love's unrequited by your number one
I wish that I hadn't waited so long to accept how I feel
Being afraid of what others would say cost me the chance at something real

I think I broke inside the day I was attacked
Ever since the three of them my odds in life have felt stacked

I let myself be used to take back some control
For those few moments I actually feel wanted, it fills the hole that's in my soul

I'm ten pounds of potatoes in a five pound bag
I've got way too much baggage, raise too many red flags
How can anyone love me until I love myself?
I've felt discarded for so long like a dusty book up on a shelf

My mother really screwed me up, my father did the rest
I never really stood a chance, even trying my best
I'm in a hellish groundhog day with no end in sight
It's why I pray I won't wake up when I close my eyes at night

I've always been a punching bag for people to abuse
Beaten down by existence and left to rot and bruise
The PTSD in my head haunts me in every way
How can I be expected to go on like this every day?

At what point does it get better, or will it never cease
Will the tide ever turn, will I ever get a release?
I'm swimming in an upstream current, my arms are fading fast
Fatigue is setting in, do I even want to last?

I thought maybe the Army would be my saving grace
Instead it was horrible- I'll never forget Top's face
He made me his whipping boy, made my life pure hell
He's a big reason why years later I can't sleep well

Let's also not forget the solider- the one I won't name
The one who took advantage of me after drinking inside and watching the rain
I thought we were good friends until you did that to me
I thought you were different but you were just like the other three.

I never could report it, you were the golden calf
I still remember laying there when you were done listening to you laugh

Thanking me for the good time that we just had
Saying you knew I wanted it and that I should be glad

As if it was a privilege to feel you inside me
Too drunk to put a stop to it or try to break free
The worst part is I liked you and on a different day
Maybe we could have done it in a more tender way

Maybe it was my fault, maybe I gave off a mood
Maybe I gave a signal when I bought drinks and made the food
Maybe I wanted it but not how it went down
Maybe I deserved it, and that's why thinking back on it makes me frown

And here now in the present I know that it's too late
I'm damaged and I'm broken, to be loveless is my fate
Even if I wanted to try time has passed me by
Middle aged head cases don't really catch anyone's eye

I keep falling for the wrong ones- letting myself catch all the feels
Desperately hoping to stumble into something real
One day I'll smarten up and maybe change my path
Instead of always getting hurt and wanting to slit my wrists in the bath

Fox In The Henhouse

I thought about you recently, though you're always on my mind
I looked you up to see what had become of you, where life had led
Do you still think about me?
Do you lie awake at night waking up in a cold sweat?
Remembering the feeling of your hot breath on my neck
The feeling of your hands holding me down
Pinning me to the locker room bench as the three of you took turns trading places
Why did I listen and follow you down there after my play rehearsal and your sports practice ended?

Do you remember the sound of your laughter, the threats that you made?
The feeling and echo of your hand slapping me across my face
Of your fingers wrapped around my throat?
Of the warm viscous fluid being spat in my face by the 3 of you as you belly laughed harder?
Of the daily groping, whispered words and threats in class,

The comments made and jokes told at my
expense for the next 2 years?

Was it good for you- it wasn't for me
And yet somehow I find myself trying to play it
out with a different end to this day
The days I still let myself be used, to try and feel
something other than the cold dead feeling I get
inside
But you imprinted on my mind that I'm just an
object to be used for your gratification and
everyone else's too

And so I had to look you up
I saw one of you was in jail- domestic abuse and
animal cruelty- Why am I not surprised?
It takes a sociopath to do the things you did to
me, and leopards never change their spots.
I can only hope that as you rot in your cell that
someone corners you in a damp shower room
Pins you down and karma and justice kick in and
you feel what I felt decades ago.
Part of me wants to visit and look you in the eye
through the glass and stand there defiant and
resolute
Showing you that I may have bent but you did
not break me.
But you aren't worth the time.

And what of the others?
One now married with a wife and kids, it's
funny what social media can show us
You get to live a happy life, though father time
hasn't been good to your looks
You don't have that wrestler's build anymore,
now you look like a stereotype of the profession
you work
So many days I considered calling that number
on your work truck
Wondering what I would say when I heard your
voice on the other end.
Dreaming about knocking on your door one day,
to look you in the eye
Maybe ring the bell on a Halloween night and
give your wife and kids a trick instead of a treat
And tell them what a monster you really are

The other working on Wall Street now, recently
divorced
I wonder if your money buys you happiness and
peace of mind
I hope it buys you soft pillows to lay on at night
Do you stare at the ceiling and think back to
what you did?
Do you even think about me ever?
When you close your eyes in that luxury condo
to go to sleep do you replay those events over
and over again in your mind?

Or do you just fade away into peaceful slumber?
I wonder what the executives of your firm would think if I ever emailed them and told them about the type of person they have working for them.
But those wolves of Wall Street probably wouldn't care and would laugh about it with you.

But as nice as dreams of revenge are it isn't worth my time.
My past will no longer define my future.
I may never forget you, or what was done, but I will heal and move on.

Friend Zone Haiku

Sitting side by side
Wishing we were holding hands
Alas-we are friends.

FTW

Sitting out here hovering in my craft
Left the world behind, that rotten vile wasteland
Saw it slowly poison itself, watched the ozone
decay as pollution went unchecked
Watched greedy corporate bastards suck dry the
teats of the poor.
Famine, Death, Plague, Pestilence all came
riding in on their stallions.
Did they see it coming?

I did, and laughed as all the nations and tribes
fell from grace
Looting, rioting, murder, rape, anarchy reigned
supreme.
I watched the White House fall, saw the Louvre
burn
The canals of Venice ran over flooding the
streets while the Artic thawed.
Flooding consumed half the world, greed and
war destroyed the rest.

Did I shed any tears as I, traveler of the stars
watched civilization fall?
Not a one.

No I, great Nero of the cosmos fiddled and
laughed as I watched it all burn.
I danced a jig, pissed on the shallow grave and
cosmic gap where the earth once was.
It never had a use for me, nor I for it.
I was hungry and never fed. Thirsty and never
satiated. Naked and never clothed.

I was the freak, the outcast, the black sheep.
Looked upon with disgust and disdain.
But being ostracized gave me time to prepare, to
see the inevitable coming.
My shuttle was prepared, ready and waiting to
take flight.
I laughed as I boarded the ship, kicking aside the
emaciated bodies crying out for help-
Begging for mercy, and I just laughed as I
continued kicking mirthfully.
And so now I sit here alone among the stars,
enjoying the tranquility as I stare into the void.
Writing my last before slipping away into the
ether, as my supplies and rations dwindle.

I, Icarus

Icarus flew too close to the sun, and now so have
I;
The fall from the heavens was worth the pain
caused by the impact of reality.

I remember the first etching of the wax
foundation-
A tap, a chat, curious eyes waiting in the dark.

Our eyes locked and I felt it in an instant- the
fire and air signs breathing life into the sparking
flame

The fire a beacon in the night, lighting the way
to those soulful eyes, blending in with the stars.

There we stood, huddled together in the cold,
making peace, and forming friendship.
Icarus and Daedalus, beginning to shape the
wings with which we'd take flight.

Who knew that lust would turn to love, a feeling
believed to be unrequited.
Always watching, always wishing; yearning for
something just out of reach.

I wanted to touch the sky, see the stars that
shaped those eyes, to hold your hand and take
flight
But we stayed grounded, for I was unconfident
in my skill as a craftsman.

Alone in the workshop I sat, sleeping each night
still dreaming about those eyes.

I practiced my craft, flying with others,
sometimes reaching the clouds, but never the
stars I desperately yearned for.

I knew only we were capable of reaching those
heights.

And still I hesitated, not wanting to anger the
gods who crossed our paths, not wishing to
tempt fate.

Afraid to lose the bond we had as we worked on
the wings time and again, inching closer to
takeoff before backing away.

We toiled away, solidifying our bond, as tight
and intricate as the wings strapped to our backs;
Finally the day came; we had the courage to
plunge off the cliff and take flight.

Soaring past the clouds, up to the heavens, defying all the warning signs, hand in hand, faster and faster, the fire and air uniting to lift the wings to heights impossible with anyone else.

And there amongst the stars, alongside you, gazing into those eyes as they shined through the cosmos, I found peace.

I found silence, stillness, I had reached Nirvana, I felt every fiber of my soul reach out and try to connect.

I wanted to give you more than the stars, I wanted to gift the sun too, something to burn as hot as the passion I felt. You deserved not just the world, but the universe as well.

I let you go back to earth while I chased that dream, waiting to see what joy the sun would bring upon my return.

I threw caution to the wind, I was inspired, ignoring the shouts of the gods who had warned me.

I pressed onward for you, feeling the heat from the sun burn as hot and fast as we did and I reached out, stretching, trying; ignoring the wax dripping down my body.

The heat of the sun and the burning in my heart was my undoing, my wings were melted and I came falling back to reality with a crash.

Broken bones will heal, but a broken spirit is harder to mend, for you were gone after our flight- back to another craftsman on another project, and I alone in my shop cleaning up the pieces and remnants of the past.

And here I sit, stoic and silent, back to watching, gazing, dreaming alone about those eyes among the stars, hoping one day to craft a better set of wings that I can take flight with again.

My Grecian Love

I see you standing there-
Breathtaking, beautiful
Venus rising form the sea
You lay veiled in innocent purity.
It's not the chaste knowledgeable Athena I want;
I want the darker, wilder corrupted Artemis
I want your love, not the feeling
But the wild hunt, the raw animalistic act
I want to be there for you, mind, body, soul
forever
Yet the curse of Hera rains upon me
For to you I don't exist
Hera's jealousy rules
I fear you look upon me and see the ugliness of
Hephaestus
The kind, noble loving god, with an unbecoming
look
I want to be Apollo and bring light into your day
I want to be your Zeus, your steadfast strong
defender
I want to kiss the salt of the sea on your lips
Taste the sea from where you came
But I do not have a chance
For thee, revered god, sees not the mere mortal

Paper Love

I saw you on that app online and had to shoot
my shot,
I know my looks weren't enough but my income
seemed to get you hot.
You're my paper love.

As we hang out together, my hardened heart
begins to crack,
It sure feels amazing when I wind up in the sack
With my paper love.

The more we get together the more I want you
bad,
I know that I'm just the emotional friend and it
makes me sad
You're the only one I want, but our lives are
worlds apart
But I can't fight these feelings, you've stolen my
heart
My paper love.

I'm good enough to hang with, or go out and eat,
Or sit by at the movies with your hand across
my seat
We stay up all hours, laughing through the night

You're the first in a long time who makes my darkness bright
But when the night is over, and it's time to say goodbye
You often turn and walk away to leave me high and dry
My paper love.

You say that I'm amazing and gaze into my eyes
You tell me I'm the sweetest but talk to other guys
I just want to lean down and kiss those soft pink lips
Instead you hug me bye at night with your arms around my hips,
You say you're attracted to my mind but something seems amiss,
If I'm so great and special why do we rarely kiss?
We only seem to wind up in bed on weeks we go out when I get paid,
It seems like it's my money and not me that gets me laid
By my paper love.

I know that I am older, and we're both on separate paths
The chances of this working seem slim when I do the math

But I just can't go back to meeting other guys
You're the only one for me, the apple of my eye,
My paper love.

I wish that I could be more for you while I'm working on myself
I want to be together, please don't keep me on the shelf.
This complicated friendship, it tears me up inside
Your love is like an airplane, a real turbulent ride
Fly with my paper love, through the skies with my paper love.

Would you still want to hang with me if I was destitute?
Would you still hug and cuddle and tell me I was cute?
Or is this all one sided, and is money at the root?
Are you just my paper love?

I love the night we go out, like when we hang out by the lake.
Are the feelings you say you have real or just fake?
Sometimes we just hang out at home and don't spend a dime
And you say you still have fun with me regardless and so I enjoy that time

With my paper love.

I know I'll never bring this up, or ask you what you think
Even if it's all shallow, you've saved me from the brink.
I don't want to lose you, even if it's all based upon a lie
I'd rather live in denial than hear the truth and want to die.

I guess that I'll just ride this out- let's see where it goes
Maybe you can love me when I fit in smaller clothes.
Until then I'll be here for you, and standing by your side,
Because to me you're worth it, going on this crazy ride
With my paper love.

Now the friendship's over, you've chosen someone else
I was tired of watching you from my place on the proverbial shelf
I'm no no one's second choice, I'm not a backup plan
But thanks for the memories and helping me find confidence in who I am
Goodbye my paper love.

The Saint of Chelsea

In an aging brownstone on 20th street
Lived the sweetest old lady one ever could meet
So many life lessons one could lean
From the saint of Chelsea named Mary Ahearn

Sharp witted and cheerful with a twinkle in her eye
Known throughout the neighborhood and all passers-by
Friend to all animals and her homeless street friends
A kind work or assistance she was always willing to lend

She opened her door to the lost when no one else would
And imparted on them confidence in a way only she could
Never judging, she only showed care
And nothing but kindness to all who stayed there

She'd feed the street needy, she'd feed the street critters
She took care of the forgotten, and never seemed bitter.

Walking miles each night with her dog in tow
This gentle old soul you'd have been lucky to
know.

Her love of puzzles and books gave her quick
wit,
With a wry sardonic sense of humor, reminiscent
of a Brit.
Celebrity neighbors and regular friends alike
All agreed they were lucky to have her in their
life.

And though she is gone, her memory remains
You won't find anybody who'd speak of her
with disdain.
I'm grateful she helped me when I needed a
home
And I still feel her spirit beside me on days
when I'm alone

Whispering in my ear a kind word or two
When I'm doubting myself or wondering what I
should do
The world would be much better if we all strived
to be
Like the kind Mary Ahearn, the Saint of
Chelsea.

Toxic

I got the news, it wasn't good. I should have known as much.
They say the world doesn't give us more than we can handle, but someone please tell the cosmos I am not Atlas, and my shoulders are weary.

And now I sit her wondering why, wondering how, wondering what could be next.

If I cut myself open and bled could I see these toxins? Could I see death flowing through my veins?

Myelocytes, promyelocytes, all these strange foreign words being thrown at me by the doctor, he may as well be speaking a foreign language

I get that diamonds are lumps of coal that have been put through pressure and exertion, but I am tired

I am weary, I am waiting to shine and wonder just how much more pressure and exertion it is going to take.

Why did I get healthy, why did I reverse the diabetes, why did I heal my liver and kidneys, just to be told I now have this running through my blood, permeating every cell inside my body.

They say it can be cured, that 20 years ago I would have been dead, but now I will live, and that is good, for I still have too much life to live

Too many plans, too much ambition, too much to struggle and fight to achieve, too many dreams unfulfilled, and yet still, nothing in life is certain but death and taxes

What if I am the 13% who does not survive?

What then, do I bemoan my fate and curse fate for dealing me a bad hand?
I want to drive into the forest, raise my fist at the stars and scream into the black void of space until my lungs have collapsed and my diaphragm is drained, until the blood rushes from my head and I collapse to my knees and begin pounding at the dirt while gnashing my teeth

But I cannot, I do not, I stay quiet and resolute like a good soldier

I maintain a brave face, a stoic demeanor, I
laugh and live a jovial existence, wearing a mask
to shield others from the fear, anger, and rage I
keep bottled up inside that I can never seem to
catch a break

Nobody likes a complainer. Nobody likes a pity
party. I too am nobody.
Even if I am fading away, feeling down
accomplishes nothing, and I remind myself of
this as the tears pour down my face and my
chest tightens, unable to breath mid anxiety
attack as I look at fragments of my life spread
out around me,

Tearing through totes looking for a book I have
misplaced, wondering what those who one day
find my cold lifeless corpse would think when
they rummage through the things I left behind
like vultures picking at the bones for any quality
meat.

But now we wait, the tests and pills are coming,
to wage an internal civil war, to fight a battle for
my life, liberty, and pursuit of happiness, Lee
and Grant in the battle of the bloodstream

Hoping that Appomattox is at the bottom of a bottle of pills and the terms of surrender are remission rather than death.
But until the final battle has been fought, the final shot has been fired, I will soldier on, stoic and resolute, leading from the front.

Hike-ku

Alone in the woods
The sound of the waterfall
Silences my mind

The Hunt

Listening to the sound of your voice
A siren's call luring me toward the rocks.
Gazing at your body, smooth and flawless
Carved from marble by Michelangelo himself.
Your soul pours forth, running in waves
Ravaging my mind with your wild currents.

I, the hunter watching you from afar.
You the elusive trophy kill I seek.
Tracking you miles through dense brush,
Watching, observing, silent as you graze.
There you sit in my crosshairs, my quest at an end;
But I cannot bring myself to shoot.

For you're too perfect, and I not deserving.
I cannot claim you for my own.
And so, heavy in heart, I lower my weapon
Shooting you with my camera instead.
Home alone I lay there gazing at your image,
Forever wondering how your flesh would have tasted.

Baba Yaga

If I wrote about him, I feel I should not neglect
you

It's you I have to thank for so much that I have

Thank you for the poor eyesight

Thank you for the PTSD, for the crippling
anxiety and mistrust in adults and other people

Whispering lies in my ears like Iago, to turn me
against all those who opposed you and your
psychosis

Thank you for trying to buy my love to
compensate for the lack of true love and
affection

Thank you for teaching me how to hate and hold
a grudge, and steel away my emotions at such a
young age

Thank you for showing me the world is scary
and unsafe as you screamed and smashed things
and waved around knives as I sat huddled under

the kitchen table screaming at the age of 4 and 5, fleeing the safety of being under the chair only so that I could go vomit from the anxiety your fights caused

Thank you for telling me you hated me and I was a mistake that should have been aborted

Thank you for choosing to run away and become a witch living in a coven on an Island before disappearing for good without saying goodbye

Thank you for disappearing from my life without a trace after wreaking havoc on it for 20 years, only to appear one final time on MSN chat during a psychotic episode to say you were kidnapped by foreign actors

Thank you for teaching me how not to treat others, and how I never want to make anybody else feel.

Thank you for being the monster I had to fear at night when trying to sleep, the one not in the closet, but hiding outside my door, Baba Yaga, a dormant volcano ready to explode at any given moment and destroy everything in it's wake.

Thank you for the parade of men in and out of life as you lived with reckless abandon, a praying mantis, a black widow, consuming them once you sucked the marrow from their bones.

Thank you for leaving me with a lifelong ability to have bile rise in the back of my throat whenever I think of you, which I've managed to do less with time.

Are you still alive?

Are you dead? You changed your name how many times, moving like a gypsy.

I considered tracking you down but ask myself why?

I will never get closure, be you alive or dead.

Instead I do my best to forget.

Blood does not make family, and your childhood was no excuse

You were evil, a narcissistic sociopath never meant to be a caregiver.

I hope you choke on the oleander you use the next time you cast your spells if you are even alive to do so, and that the poison causes you excruciating agony as it courses through your veins in a botched attempt to wield the unworldly power you always craved.

I thank you for forcing me to grow up so fast and harden my heart, and how to be a survivor.

And lastly, I thank you to finally leave my mind and give me peace, and stop haunting my dreams.

www.ingramcontent.com/pod-product-compliance
Lightning Source LLC
Chambersburg PA
CBHW062202160726
48282CB00027B/962
9789357618182